Why you should join the socialists

by Paul Foot
with cartoons by Tim Sanders

BOOKMARKS
London, Chicago, Melbourne

Why you should join the socialists / *Paul Foot*
Published November 1993
Bookmarks, 265 Seven Sisters Road, London N4 2DE
Bookmarks, PO Box 16085, Chicago, Il. 60616
Bookmarks, GPO Box 1473N, Melbourne 3001
ISBN 0 906224 80 2
© Bookmarks and Paul Foot
Printed by Cox and Wyman Ltd, Reading

Bookmarks is linked to an international grouping of socialist organisations:

AUSTRALIA: **International Socialist Organisation,**
GPO Box 1473N, Melbourne 3001

BELGIUM: **Socialisme International,**
Rue Lovinfosse 60, 4030 Grevignée

BRITAIN: **Socialist Workers Party,**
PO Box 82, London E3 3LH

CANADA: **International Socialists,**
PO Box 339, Station E, Toronto, Ontario M6H 4E3

CYPRUS: **Workers Democracy,**
PO Box 7280, Nicosia, Cyprus

DENMARK: **Internationale Socialister,**
Postboks 642, 2200 København, N

FRANCE: **Socialisme International,**
BP 189, 75926 Paris, Cedex 19

GERMANY: **Sozialistische Arbeitersgruppe,**
Wolfsgangstrasse 81, W-6000, Frankfurt 1

GREECE: **Organosi Sosialistiki Epanastasi,**
PO Box 8161, 10010, Omonia, Athens

HOLLAND: **Groep Internationale Socialisten,**
PO Box 9720, 3506 GR Utrecht

IRELAND: **Socialist Workers Movement,**
PO Box 1648, Dublin 8

NEW ZEALAND: **International Socialist Organisation,**
PO Box 6157, Dunedin

NORWAY: **Internasjonale Sosialister,**
Postboks 9226, Grønland 0134, Oslo

POLAND: **Solidarnosc Socjalistyczna,**
PO Box 12, 01-900 Warszawa 118

SOUTH AFRICA: **International Socialists of South Africa,**
PO Box 18530, Hillbrow 2038

UNITED STATES: **International Socialist Organisation,**
PO Box 16085, Chicago, Il. 60616

Contents

Paul Foot has been a member of the Socialist Workers Party and its predecessor, the International Socialists, since 1962. He was editor of *Socialist Worker* in 1974 and 1975 and wrote *Why You Should be a Socialist* in 1977. In 1990, he wrote *The Case for Socialism*. His other books include *Red Shelley* (1981), *Immigration and British Politics* (1965) and *The Politics of Harold Wilson* (1968). A collection of his articles from the *Daily Mirror*, *The London Review of Books*, *Socialist Worker* and *Socialist Review* was published in *Words as Weapons* (1990).

A world in chaos

WILL YOUR children have a better life than you? If you'd been asked that question at any other time in the last 50 years, the answer would have been a certain 'Yes'. After the Second World War, the defeat of fascism, the formation of the United Nations and what looked like full employment in the whole of the industrial world, there was hardly anyone anywhere who did not feel that at last human beings had come to their senses. 'Never again!' was the universal cry. No more fascism. No more mass poverty. No more unemployment. No more wars.

In Britain this optimism lasted through the post-war Labour government of 1945-1951. Even when the Tories came, in they didn't bring a slump with them. All through the 1950s and 1960s almost everyone could get a job. The trade unions grew big and strong. Though the Tories didn't like the National Health Service when Labour brought it in, they didn't dismantle it. The NHS was almost completely free for its first 25 years. Huge new hospitals were built, with the

7

most modern equipment, and opened to the whole public.

The Tory governments of the 1950s and early 1960s built hundreds of thousands of council houses at rents which most people could afford. In the 1960s and 1970s, most secondary schools became comprehensives. The old barbarian division between secondary modern schools for the majority and snob grammar schools for the middle class was done away with. A huge host of new universities were built for a new wave of students, every single one of whom believed as their parents did that their children would be better off, better educated, better housed and better employed than they were.

This optimism survived the disappointments of the 1970s. Now, however, it has disappeared.

On all sides there is gloom about the present and pessimism about the future. When asked about their children's prospects, parents prefer to hope rather than predict. They hope things will get better, but they doubt it.

In 1976, unemployment reached one and a half million; in 1983, nearly three million; now the official figures, grotesquely massaged by the Tories, are up to three million again.

Everyone who has a job has found they work harder and longer. The small pleasures of the workplace—breaks, conversation, recreation—are all dying. Speed-ups, having to do someone else's job—these are the constant instructions of a new breed of ruthless employers.

Many of those NHS hospitals built in the 1960s are earmarked for closure. Council flats built in the 1960s are being pulled down.

The number of council houses built in 1981 was 45,948. This slumped, incredibly, to 8,073 in 1991. Capital spending on council houses in 1982 was £2.9bn; in 1992 (after allowing for inflation) it had fallen to £1.5bn. This has been hailed by the Tories as proof of a property owners' democracy. 'More and more people are buying their homes, so they don't need houses to rent' trumpeted the Tories.

But the high interest rates demanded by the mortgage companies in the late 1980s and early 1990s led to

Why you should join the socialists

a new tyranny: the tyranny of the moneylender. Between 1989 and 1992, more than a hundred thousand families lost their homes to the moneylenders. Those who managed to cling on fell deeper and deeper into debt. In the 1970s, debt was the equivalent of less than a quarter of the average family's annual income. Today it is a staggering 92 percent.

The disparity between rich and poor has grown enormously in the last ten years.

The statistics are frightening. At the beginning of the 1980s, 1 percent of the British population was classified as living below the poverty line. By the same guidelines, that figure has now grown to 21 percent. The bottom fifth of the population earned nearly 10 percent of all income in 1979. Today they earn 6.3 percent, while the top 20 percent have increased their share from 37 percent to a fantastic 45 percent. The poorest grew much poorer, the richest much richer.

Traditionally high standards of public amenities in Britain's cities have almost everywhere been abandoned. Roads in poor areas are not maintained, parks are vandalised, welfare centres and old peoples' clubs closed.

Those who do not collapse in despair take to crime. Again, the chief victims are the poor.

Mentally ill people, increasing in number with the social chaos around them, sleep in city streets. The whole of our society, so hopeful and confident in the 25 years after the war, now seems to be disintegrating.

This is not a British problem. The same disintegration is going on all over the world. One in ten of the world's population will never be able to answer any question about their children. They are the 500 million people, most of them under the age of five, who will not survive to child-bearing age because they don't get enough to eat.

A world in chaos

In the 1950s and 1960s United Nations economic experts believed they could win what one of them called 'The War on World Poverty'. Now no one believes that. No one believes that the crucifying poverty of at least a quarter of the world's people is ever going to be relieved. The only question now is how soon another billion people will be added to the billion already starving.

Whole tracts of the world, especially in Africa and South East Asia, are each year abandoned to drought and famine. In Rio de Janeiro the authorities have found an answer to the problem of parentless children who, in their thousands, scrape a living in the city streets. They send out death squads to kill them. In Bolivia the starving children cannot even get to the cities: 97 percent of the rural population of that beautiful and blighted country are living below the (very mean) UN poverty line.

Old diseases, like cholera in Peru or tuberculosis in Tower Hamlets, and new diseases like AIDS, are ensuring the premature deaths of more and more of the starving millions who are lucky enough to survive death by starvation in their childhood.

Famine, Disease and Death were three of the Four Horsemen of the Apocalypse, who, according to the Bible in about AD 70, and the general secretary of the UN in 1961, threaten one day to conquer the earth. Today, after 2,000 years of progress, all three are shepherding us to the rim of hell.

The fourth horseman was War.

When the UN was set up in 1946, people hoped it would once and for all put a stop to war. When Russia and the US simultaneously developed weapons of mass destruction which could wipe out the entire world many times over, we cowered for nearly 50 years under the threat of a nuclear holocaust which would wipe out the human race. When Russia and her empire collapsed in the late 1980s, the confident prediction of Western academics was that the end of the Cold War would lead to an end of all wars.

In 1989, the American historian Francis Fukuyama forecast an eternity of liberal peace. Before the ink was dry on his book, the peace-keeping United Nations

10

themselves declared war on Iraq. This Gulf War killed, on a conservative estimate, 30,000 Iraqi citizens, most of them people who had nothing but loathing and hatred for their dictator, Saddam Hussein. Saddam himself survived.

George Bush, the US president who used the United Nations as his own fiefdom, suggested that his Gulf War victory would end all wars. It would usher in, he promised, a 'New World Order'.

How has the 'New World Order' been shaping up? All over the world new, monstrous wars based in the main on national divisions which have absolutely no relevance to the well-being of the people involved have turned whole countries into slaughter houses.

What used to be Yugoslavia has been pulverised by a ghastly civil war between Serbs, Croats and Bosnian Muslims who have lived side by side without conflict for decades.

Huge and horrible wars have broken out in the former republics of the USSR—in Azerbaijan, in Georgia and Tadzhikistan. In Angola, Afghanistan, Liberia, Somalia, the Sudan and many other places, civil wars are being waged whose pointlessness is as outrageous as their

11

A world in chaos

cruelties. The New World Order is grimmer even than the Cold War.

Why? Even the most long-suffering people are asking why. From the people in charge of society they get three answers.

Blame the weather

THE FIRST ANSWER, which comes strangely from those who tell us they are our rulers, is that they, the rulers, are not in charge at all. To all this poverty and war, they say, there are no possible remedies.

Thus for the whole of the latest recession, the British prime minister, John Major, and his chancellors of the exchequer, said that unemployment was 'a world-wide phenomenon' which they were powerless to control.

The same argument was used by Prime Ministers and their treasurers everywhere else. The recession, it was said, started somewhere else. It was like the weather—like a depression which had mysteriously started somewhere over Greenland, and had swept from there to Britain and the rest of the world. No one can stop a hurricane, we were reminded, and similarly no one can stop a recession.

Politicians who pretend they are in charge of every other aspect of human society insist that as far as the most important issue is concerned, the economic well-being of the citizens they aspire to represent, they are not in charge at all. They resort to biblical metaphors, to the parable of the seven lean years and the seven fat years, and blame poor old God for all the disasters which encompass us. The people have sinned, say these soothsayers, and God is paying them back. What further proof is required of His omnipotence?

The socialist answer is that human beings can decide what happens to them. They can act to determine their destiny. This is what separates us from the rest of the animal world. We need not be tossed around by unpredictable forces of nature or of anything else. The idea that human beings can send one another to the moon, can conquer the mysteries of outer space, can control and harness the power of the rivers, seas and mountains and yet cannot control the simplest problems affecting their livelihood is plainly absurd.

Human nature

THE SECOND argument starts with the assumption that human beings are naturally evil, that they are always fighting each other (hence the wars), that they are lazy (hence the unemployment) and that they are greedy and selfish (hence the gap between rich and poor).

All the evidence suggests, however, that people do not want to be at war and they certainly don't want to be unemployed. The overwhelming majority of people prefer peace to war, full employment to unemployment.

In the period following the Second World War there was full employment all over the industrial world. All those apparently lazy people suddenly started working, and were much happier working than they were when they were on the dole. Moreover, very large numbers of people, then and now, if they are faced with a straight alternative of working for a low wage or living idle on slightly lower benefits, prefer to work than to be idle.

Almost every war ever fought, whatever the popular enthusiasm for it when it started, has ended in widespread popular discontent and anger.

If anything, therefore, human nature is against unemployment and against war.

What about greed and selfishness? Certainly there

13

are plenty of examples of both. But there are also plenty of examples of generosity and selflessness too. Every donation to charity, every factory collection for a disabled child, every visit to donate blood—all these and countless other examples show what we know to be the case—that virtually all of us can be selfish and/or selfless, greedy and/or generous. The point is: which side of these two aspects of human nature is encouraged or discouraged?

The poor are always with us

THIS ARGUMENT is attributed to Jesus Christ. Nothing has more comforted the rich followers of the humble carpenter than this quotation. It means that whatever we do, there will always be poverty. The reason, the argument goes on, is that there is never enough to go round. Some people are always going to get the gravy, while others are always going to starve.

In Year One, there was something to be said for this argument. While Jesus Christ was reported to be spelling out his egalitarian ideas among the dispossessed in Judea, there wasn't enough to go round. Either a few people at the top became rich and had some leisure, or no one did. So the people at the top justified their riches on the grounds that their leisure and culture was better than no leisure and no culture. There would be neither, they claimed, if their wealth was taken away from them and shared equally among everyone.

To this day, rich people comfort themselves with this ancient belief that the starving millions would starve anyway, that there is still nothing like enough to go round.

Their argument has been out of date for at least 150 years. There is more than enough to go round.

There is enough food produced to feed everyone on earth. That is not a wild exaggeration. It is the simple truth spelled out every year by all sorts of organisations, in particular the United Nations Food and Agricultural Organisation (FAO). If all the surplus food now rotting in granaries or food mountains were distributed to the hungry, no one would starve. Moreover, with a little bit of scientific application to food production, there could be much more.

14

In 1976, the FAO announced in its annual report that there would be 'no difficulty', given the current state of knowledge about food production, in doubling world food production. Another expert said that if world food production was organised as it is in Holland, as it could be for relatively small investment, there would be enough food to feed 67 billion people—15 times the entire world's population.

Instead of finding ways to distribute the food they produce, the people who decide these things spend more and more time trying to cut food production down. In Britain a brilliant new scheme has been devised called 'set aside' in which farmers are paid by the taxpayer not to produce food. The British government, which is always complaining about how little money it has, dished out £26m last year to farmers to stop them producing food. The aim, we were told, was to take a third of the arable land in Britain out of production. While the starving millions increase, the people who control agriculture are making a nice living out of reducing food production.

It's the same story with all the basic necessities of life. In Britain there are more than enough houses for the homeless. It is just that many of the excess houses are empty—or the second, third and even the fourth houses of rich people who like everyone else can only live in one place at any one time.

All round is proof that the poor need not always be with us: that poverty and hunger co-exist with vast unused resources which could end all poverty and hunger tomorrow.

Indeed, if we stopped making useless and dangerous things and switched those resources to safe and

CASH CROP NOT FIT FOR HUMAN CONSUMPTION

A world in chaos

useful things, the world's people could get not just what they need but also what they want.

Here's another calculation from world agriculture experts. If 0.5 percent of the world's enormous spending on weapons was diverted to agriculture in Africa, the murderous poverty which threatens to engulf at least three quarters of that continent's population would immediately be lifted. The agricultural investment necessary, the machinery, the replenishing of the soil and all the other conditions for a booming African agriculture could be fulfilled—almost overnight. Half of one percent! It seems a miserable demand.

Yet year by year the amount spent on arms goes up while the amount set aside for investment in African agriculture goes down. The British arms industry slaps itself on the back for exporting £26bn worth of weapons, while the percentage of the national product spent on aid to the poor went down and down from 0.5 in 1987 to 0.3 in 1992.

All three familiar arguments used by people to justify the world we live in don't stand up to a moment's investigation. Human beings are not helpless puppets manipulated constantly by nature, religious forces or anything else. They are in control.

•*It's obviously not human nature to be unemployed or to go to war*—or that 1 percent of the people should have a quarter of all the wealth.

•*The poor need not be with us*—there is absolutely no need for anyone in the world to be starving.

There is enough food for the hungry—so why don't they get it? There are enough homes for the homeless, so why don't they live in them? Why do the food mountains grow as fast as the hunger queues, the numbers of homeless millions as fast as the numbers of empty homes or surplus bricks? Why does the world get worse, when its capacity to make everything better improves all the time?

These are the questions to which people need straight answers.

16

The robbers and the robbed

SITTING AT the top of every society on earth is a handful of rich people. They are so much richer than the rest of us that we cannot imagine their wealth. On the latest reckoning 5 percent of British adults, about one and a quarter million people, got 50 percent of all the income earned by everyone in the country. When wealth (not just income) is measured, the same 5 percent own 75 percent of everything there is to own.

There's nothing specially British, or even Western about these fantastic inequalities. The poorer the country, the more grotesque the differences in wealth and income. President Mobutu, for instance, the dictator of Zaire, one of the poorest countries on earth, has a personal fortune worth hundreds of millions of dollars.

NATURALLY WE NEED MUCH MORE MONEY THAN YOU, BECAUSE OUR APPETITE FOR LUXURY IS SO MUCH HARDER TO SATISFY.

How have these rich people become rich? Their apologists argue that wealth is a measure of ability: that people are rich because they are better, more able, more enterprising, more dynamic than others in society and that therefore they deserve their riches.

17

In fact, most rich people owe their wealth not to anything they have done, but to inheritance. They are rich because their fathers or grandfathers, in a tremendous spurt of initiative and enterprise, died, leaving a fortune to their successors.

Even the minority of the rich who have become rich in their lifetime can seldom point to any specially brilliant ability. Robert Maxwell, for instance, the archetypal tycoon, was always ascribing his own riches to his brilliant managerial skills. In fact, he was a rotten manager. He never trusted anyone enough to delegate to them any decision. He took all decisions himself, forgetting all the time which ones he'd taken. He made his fortune from publishing, but he himself could hardly read. He insisted that every written communication to him should be reduced to a single sentence, and highlighted. He was an ignoramus, a buffoon, a strutting bully of no use to anyone. But he made millions.

Robert Maxwell is an unfair example, you might say. He was a crook. So let's consider someone from the same time and the same industry who is not a crook. Andrew Knight is the chief executive of the British arm of News Corporation, the biggest media company in the world. Before that he was chief executive of the *Daily Telegraph*. When he took office at the *Telegraph* he was given some share options. When News Corporation took over, they agreed to compensate him for his share options. So one fine day Andrew Knight received £14m.

Andrew Knight was once a rather unexciting editor of the *Economist*. He is well informed and undoubtedly efficient. There are thousands of others equally well-informed and efficient. But one day Andrew got £14m. That wasn't down to any effort on his part or any special contribution. And it wasn't even just a question of one rather dull man becoming a millionaire. All the little Andrew Knights are already millionaires too.

Perhaps Andrew got his fortune by luck, rather like winning the pools. But this doesn't explain his wealth either. Everyone knows where the money for pools winners comes from. It comes from other people who have bet on the pools, and understand quite well that the winner is going to pocket the losing bets. Andrew Knight wasn't betting. His £14m didn't come from other peoples' bets.

Don't think Andrew Knight was something very special. Every generation throws up a host of Andrew Knights—and the 1980s threw up more such people than any decade before it. Only a tiny proportion of these rich people can point to an invention or any contribution to human society which explains their wealth. For every rich person who can say he or she has invented or contributed something special to the society, there are scores if not hundreds of others who can't give a single social explanation for why they are so rich.

Let's have a look at the statistics of the wealthy to see if we can find out how they got rich. These statistics, by the way, are few and thin. The rich don't like people talking about their wealth—they regard it as rather vulgar.

Most people get all or most of their wealth from wages or salaries. A few people get rich from their salaries. For instance, in May 1993 the chief executive of an insurance company called Direct Line, a Mr Norman Wood, had his salary raised to £18m a year. The company proudly announced that this amounted to £36 a minute. A swift calculation showed that this included the hours that Mr Wood spent asleep. When people start earning money when they are asleep, then they can't really attribute their riches to their own brilliance or their own effort.

Ridiculous salaries like that of Mr Wood are very exceptional. They don't help us very much with our question: why are people rich? The answer to that question comes when you look at that part of rich peoples' wealth which has nothing to do with their job or any work they do. This is called unearned income.

The Treasury reveals that in 1992, £6.6bn of *unearned income* went into the pockets of the top 1 percent of British taxpayers, that's just 247,000 people. £6.6bn! That's between 3 and 4 percent of everything which is produced in Britain just sliding in a single year into the pockets of the mega-rich in return for no work, no effort, no contribution, nothing!

Where did the money come from? It came from rent, other people renting offices or houses they owned;

19

interest, existing money which grows when they put it in a bank or a building society; or dividends, which come from shares which they own in companies.

These rich people are the first to protest that they are not the only people who make money from rent, interest or dividends. That's true. Lots of people (though much fewer than is usually pretended in the newspapers of the rich) make a little money from having some savings in a building society or buying shares perhaps in a newly-privatised industry they work in. But the vast bulk, more than 85 percent, of all this 'unearned income' is available only to a tiny minority at the top of society. If you count all these people's families and dependents, they are no more than two million people.

How do these two million manage to corner the market for unearned income? Why can't we all get a whiff

20

of it? The answer is that this tiny minority own the means of producing things, the means of financing things and the means of distributing things. That is, they own the offices, houses, building societies, factories, banks, stores, oil, gas, electricity, water. They own almost everything where goods are produced, transported, distributed, bought and sold. From this ownership they derive their dividends, their rents and their interest. They cream off a surplus for themselves.

That surplus is, quite literally, stolen from the people who do the work. If nobody did any work, if there was no production or distribution, there would be no wealth. There wouldn't be any wages or salaries, and there certainly wouldn't be any unearned income. The source of all wealth is people's work. Wages and salaries obviously come from work. Less obviously, but no less directly, unearned income derives from work. It goes to people who do no work from people who do all the work.

The name for this is exploitation. People often use that word to describe something specially dreadful. It conjures up a picture of a fat very rich man (rather like Robert Maxwell) bathing in the sweat of his workers. But the truth is that exploitation goes on all the time. Every minute of every day rich people are growing richer through their unearned income, whose origin is someone else's work. This is the economic and social system called capitalism: a system run entirely by vampires.

The human vampires at the top of our society know perfectly well where their riches come from. They know that they have no real right to all that unearned income, but they plan to hang onto it forever. Their ill-gotten gains drive them together. They form solid ranks with one another, entertain one another, speak to one another in peculiar accents. They are always ready to welcome into their number new recruits from the lower orders. Indeed, these new recruits often turn out to be the most ruthless defenders of their swag—as well as proof positive that 'anyone can be rich'.

They make up a class, which pretends all the time that they hate the concept of class. Their wealth ensures that. They are forever nervous that their wealth might be

The robbers and the robbed

snatched from them by the people from whom they steal it, so they club together to protect themselves and their property.

They help pay for a whole state machinery which ensures that their property is physically protected by laws, judges and the police. They run newspapers and television stations to ensure that the ideas which float about in society correspond to their own. They devise a system of education which ensures that their sons and daughters, whatever their ability, will be able to qualify for the ranks of their class when they grow up. They form 'public schools' from which the public is excluded, and universities which give priority to those same public school students. Even today, after years and years of so-called democratic advance, more than half the pupils at the two top universities, Oxford and Cambridge, went to an expensive 'public school'.

These are not crude assertions. They are forged in the statistics and backgrounds of the people who run the state: the industrialists, bankers, civil servants, senior police officers, the judges, media moguls, generals and admirals. Everywhere the naked class bias is plain to anyone who cares to look.

The fact that this rich class is in control, and that its chief aim is the siphoning off of a surplus from the people who do the work, explains the crazinesses of the world we live in.

Why is there enough food rotting in a granary in Lancashire to feed the whole population of Somalia for a year? Because the people who produce food—the fat mega-farmers, the distributors and the merchants—are interested in producing food only if they can make a profit out of it. The people of Somalia don't have the money to buy it at the price necessary to make a profit, so they don't get the food. Instead, governments conveniently devise schemes whereby the taxpayers pay those farmers profitable prices for their food, and then store any surplus in granaries.

How is it possible that a homeless man in London in January 1993 had to have his legs amputated after sleeping out in the cold, when there are enough bricks stored

22

in the country to build twice as many houses as were built in Britain last year? Because the people in charge of brick production and house building only produce for profit. Our amputee has no job, so he can't pay for a mortgage to buy a house. So the bricks are stacked in fields, a quarter of a million building workers are out of a job and the homeless freeze.

Why is 13 percent of the income of the United States devoted to a system of health care which is far less efficient and health-giving than in Britain, where only 5 percent of the national income goes on health? Because in the US health care is mainly a profit-making business.

Why were the public utilities in Britain—water, electricity, gas and telephones—privatised? Is any one of these utilities remotely better than when it was owned by the government? Certainly not. They are run, almost all of them, by the same people and in the same way as they were before they were privatised. The only difference is that a few people, mainly rich people, now make enormous sums of money from dividends.

The rich and the Tory government say the sale of lots of shares to people who are not rich is a big boost for democracy. This is nonsense. A few non-rich people buy shares, and sell them instantly at a tiny profit, leaving the vast majority of shares in the hands of the same rich minority, and the pension funds and insurance companies which they exclusively control. What little democracy there was in these industries—a minister had to answer for them in the House of Commons—has completely disappeared.

Why were buses de-regulated when every single statistic shows that de-regulation leads to higher fares and

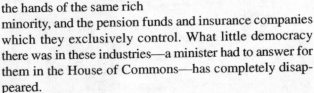

The robbers and the robbed

fewer journeys? Since de-regulation there have been fare increases averaging 30 percent and, by coincidence, a fall-off in passenger journeys of 30 percent. In Sheffield, since de-regulation, half the people who used to travel by bus now do not do so. Most of them find it difficult to travel at all. Why? Because individuals are now, for the first time, making profit and dividends from buses which were previously publicly owned.

Why is government policy on transport founded on the motor car, which transports people far more expensively and infinitely more dangerously than trains or buses? Because there is more profit in lots of cars rushing around guzzling petrol and fouling up the environment than there is in trains or buses.

Why is cannabis, endlessly tested without the slightest sign that it causes anyone any harm, illegal and hounded throughout the 'civilised' world, while tobacco, which causes a thousand times more deaths even than heroin, is openly flouted and advertised throughout society? Because there is legal profit in tobacco, only dangerous and illegal profit in cannabis.

In October 1992, the British government announced it was closing down half the coal industry. The reason, it said, was that there was no 'demand' for the power which would be fuelled by the coal. If there was no demand, they said, there was no point in keeping the capacity. So the pits had to close.

At the same time as the closures were announced,

24

a huge programme was started to expand the capacity for power. Literally alongside the closed coal-fired power stations, new gas-fired power stations were built all over the country. Yet gas-fired power is, by every account, more expensive than coal-fired power. Why, then, not use the old coal-fired stations, hold prices down and keep the pits open?

Answer: the new gas-fired power stations and their construction companies have a new set of private shareholders, providing a new source of dividends for the rich. Into the bargain, the new power stations have much weaker trade unions than the National Union of Mineworkers.

Why did the West go to war against Saddam Hussein when he attacked Kuwait in 1990? They said it was to smash an aggressor. But there have been plenty of aggressors before and since—Indonesia in East Timor, Israel in the Lebanon, Turkey in Cyprus and many others. What was the difference? The difference is that Kuwait produces 8 percent of the world's oil and the profits of the oil companies were threatened by the toppling of their friendly dictator-Emir.

The whole world is full of madnesses and contradictions like these. Every one of them can be explained by an economic system run to enrich a small wealthy minority at the expense of everyone else.

The rich, as we've seen, club together. They form themselves into a class, and they know they have a common interest. Because they are a minority, this class behaves in an entirely undemocratic fashion. Democracy is a threat to them. It threatens the entirely undemocratic source of their wealth. Industrialists and bankers, for instance, are not elected. Judges are not elected. Neither are newspaper proprietors, top civil servants, police or army chiefs. All their organisations work by a mysterious system of 'appointment' at the top and a ruthless hierarchical system of control all the way to the bottom. Everything happens by command, nothing by consent. Even the Tory Party, the instrument through which the British rich get their representatives elected into parliament, has no democracy. Its chairman and executive are not elected. Its con-

25

ference has no votes. The whole class from top to bottom yields to ancestral voices calling for order, loyalty and patriotism.

The people who do the work are also a class. Just as the robbers have a common interest, so do the robbed. Like their employers, the workers form their organisations to protect themselves. But workers have little or no individual wealth or power, they need to come together and pool their resources, so democracy comes naturally to them. Their organisations are founded on democratic choice. Trade unions elect their officers. Their conferences are made up of elected delegates, who discuss their policy. When the Labour Party was formed to represent trade unions in parliament, it set up a democratic structure. For a time, the party did not even have a leader. Even today the Labour Party elects its chairperson and executive, and, in theory at any rate, discusses and decides policy at a democratic conference.

The central characteristic of our society is the tussle between these two classes, between the greedy hierarchy of the rulers and the fumbling democracy of the workers. The language of class warfare is, however, unfashionable. The rich like to pretend that they have no interest in class. They say that they owe their riches to their own brilliance. They pretend to care about the poor and sick, and boast constantly of their philanthropy. Class language is sometimes unfashionable among workers too, who often prefer to believe the word of 'important' people.

Despite the fact that very few people refer to it, the class struggle goes on all the same, like a ceaselessly ebbing and flowing tide. The type of world we live in depends very much on how that struggle is going, on which side is winning.

How has the struggle gone in Britain since the end of the Second World War? From 1945-1975, our side, the workers' side, was relatively strong. Almost everyone had a job, and trade unions grew. The employers and their class got weaker. By 1972, when a miners' strike broke the Tories' pay policy and a threatened general strike broke its anti-union laws, the government were panicking. There was wild talk of political coups, about na-

26

tional governments and the need for private armies to defend the rich and their property. In 1973, at Christmas time, the Secretary of State for Industry, John Davies, called his family together and told them this was the last Christmas they could expect to spend in the manner to which they were accustomed. Dark clouds of egalitarianism, freedom and democracy lowered on every side.

The counter-attack for the rich was led by Margaret Thatcher, who was elected leader of the Tory Party in 1975. It started at an intellectual level, in suddenly-sprouting right wing institutes and think-tanks: the Institute of Economic Affairs, the Centre for Policy Studies and the new vibrant alternative to the Confederation of British Industry, the Institute of Directors.

These organisations spread wide the gospel for private enterprise. The aim was to win the class war for the rich and their allies. This had to be done not just in the 'hearts and minds' of the people but in open struggle with the trade unions.

Still protesting publicly that class was out of date, Thatcher and Co plotted a class war of the most subtle and savage variety. The man in charge was her trusted lieutenant, Nicholas Ridley. Ridley had been sacked from the Heath Tory government because he was too right wing. He was taken into Thatcher's inner circle in 1975, and worked on an industrial battle-plan to redress the class forces in British society.

27

The robbers and the robbed

The Ridley plan was leaked to the *Economist* in 1978. Its theme was the breaking of trade union power by open struggle on the class battlefield. Ridley proposed to start by provoking and beating a strike against a weak union in a nationalised industry—he suggested steel. This should be followed by open class warfare against the railway unions. Finally, if and when such strategies were successful, he proposed a concerted effort against the real enemy: the miners.

As soon as the Tories won the 1979 election, this plan was put into effect. The Thatcherite guru Sir Keith Joseph was put in charge of 'trade and industry'.

One of his first appointments was Ian McGregor, a dour and dedicated class warrior from the American merchant bank, Lazards Freres, as chairman of British Steel, the nationalised company which owned almost all British steel plants. At once McGregor set about mass sackings, contemptuously ignoring the unions which had been used for years to close negotiations.

28

The sackings prompted precisely the strike which Ridley had planned. The steel union leaders, quite unused to this sort of battle, consistently sabotaged the efforts of the rank and file to spread the strike. They rolled over on their backs and surrendered. The steel industry was then ripe for systematic sackings, plunder and privatisation.

In the same year, 1980, the Tories introduced the first of a long string of anti-trade union laws, whose chief effect was to outlaw all solidarity action, and so to isolate all future strikes. Any union which disobeyed the law could have its entire funds 'sequestered', or confiscated.

The Ridley plan was carried out to the letter. It was not always successful. For instance, in 1981 the Minister of Energy, David Howell, tentatively suggested that 50 coal mines should be closed. Rank and file miners, without even waiting for a call from their union, responded with a series of unofficial strikes which threatened in days to engulf the whole industry. The Tories withdrew. The 50-pit closure plan was scrapped, and David Howell, a symbol in Thatcher's eyes of a defeat for her class, was sacked, never again to return to government.

After that brief set-back, the Ridley plan went smoothly. The railway unions were next in line. There followed a long and bitter dispute with them over government-inspired plans by British Rail to speed up the rostering of engine drivers. In 1983, McGregor was shifted from chairman of British Steel to the same post at British Coal. In the same year, the Tories were returned with a huge majority and at once started plans for their biggest battle.

In early 1984, McGregor began to close pits without consultation with the miners' union. The immediate reply was a strike in every major coalfield except Nottingham. This strike was not the pushover the Ridleyites had enjoyed in steel. The miners' union was led by fighters who consistently defied the law on picketing and secondary action. At least twice in the first few months of the strike it looked like winning, chiefly through the support of railway workers and dockers. In desperation, the Tories paid off the two other unions.

The police, hugely overpaid in generous overtime payments, were co-ordinated for the first time under a national anti-strike unit. The media were roused to fantastic crescendos of hate against the miners' leaders. The Tories' greatest asset was the scabbing of miners in Nottingham and the reluctance of the TUC and the Labour Party leadership to join in the miners' fight. Pleading as ever their belief in 'constitutional change' and ridiculing any notion of class warfare, both these organisations warned their supporters against 'direct action'. At last, after 12 months of struggle and hardship from the miners, and fantastic extravagance on the part of the government, the strike was defeated. The old enemy had been conquered.

In the ten years since, the wounded NUM has been pursued with the most relentless savagery. Nothing will satisfy the rich save the destruction of the entire coal mining industry.

The immediate result of the miners' defeat was the confidence it inspired in the newspaper proprietors, who faced perhaps the toughest trade unions of all. The vulnerability of Britain's newspapers to sit-ins and lightning strikes had built up a huge union power base in the print.

Print workers had reduced the arrogance and confidence of the old proprietors. They had been prominent in all the great struggles to keep trade unions strong: in particular the battle against *In Place of Strife*, an anti-union measure introduced by the Labour government in 1969, and in the Pentonville dockers' victory in 1972.

The proprietors plotted to end trade unions in the print. In 1983, they had pushed a bewildered small buccaneer called Eddie Shah into the firing line, urging him to take on the unions at Warrington. When Shah had been used for their purposes, the proprietors cast him aside.

After the defeat of the miners, the proprietors became even more aggressive. In January 1985, in a carefully-organised manoeuvre, backed to the hilt by the Metropolitan Police, Rupert Murdoch closed down all his printing operations in Fleet Street and moved his four big national papers, the *Times* and *Sunday Times*, the *News of the World* and the *Sun*, to Wapping. He sacked all his unionised printworkers and hired scabs. The protests and pickets which followed were defeated. There was no solidarity action on other papers, and effectively the golden era of trade unionism in the print was over.

30

Liberal journalists who had felt professional distaste for horny handed trade unionism in the print predicted that the end of the 'dictatorship' of the trade unions in newspapers would lead to many more newspapers (since they were so much cheaper to produce) and a greater flow of information.

Nothing of the sort happened. The one newspaper to have started after Wapping which has survived—*The Independent*—is, as this is written, in serious financial difficulties. The *Sunday Correspondent* died a quick death. *Today*, the paper of the proud Eddy Shah, was gobbled up by Murdoch. The papers became, by any measure, even more slavish to their masters than they were previously. The only real change was in the profits of the proprietors which rose to quite fantastic proportions.

The ten years since the miners' strike have reflected, almost without exception, the rulers' victory in that battle. The Tories have twice been returned to office. The privatisation plunder went on and on—telephones, gas, electricity, water. Now even railways are under threat, if any way can be found to squeeze profit from that already run-down industry.

Another institution hated by the Tories, since it puts people's needs first and brings large numbers of unionised workers together in a collective effort to improve the lot of their fellow human beings, is the National Health Service. So popular is the NHS that Thatcher once declared 'the National Health Service is safe with us'. Holding high that banner, the Tories have been privatising the NHS by the back-door. New NHS trusts, operating on the profit motive and stuffed with Tory estate agents, property speculators, furniture manufacturers and party hacks, have been set up to bring 'commercial values' to an institution whose strength derived from its contempt for commercial values. Hospitals are encouraged to compete with one another for equipment and expertise,

I DON'T REMEMBER HAVING A POSTAL BALLOT ABOUT CLOSING THE FACTORY.

31

The robbers and the robbed

and charge each other accordingly. Doctors, who also supported the NHS, were encouraged to enrich themselves and their practises at the expense of others by becoming fundholders and achieving a 'fast track' to treatment for their patients.

A two-tier health service emerged in which patients from middle class areas where the fundholders flourish could jump the health queue.

Exactly the same process was encouraged in the state schools. Middle class, former grammar schools were bribed to 'opt out', to cut away from the elected local authorities and to set themselves up as individual capitalist units, funded directly by the government. Once again, the criterion for a good school was not teaching standards, still less the successful teaching of disabled, handicapped or 'special needs' pupils (all of whom were increasingly thrown on the rubbish heap), but dear old profitability.

In keeping with the traditions of their class, the Tories encouraged across the whole face of society a disengagement from democracy. Pretending all the time that they detested bureaucracy, they ensured that more and more of British life was controlled by bureaucrats.

The slender threads by which elected local authorities, community health councils and the like maintained a semblance of social accountability were systematically snapped. Local councils were overburdened with jobs they couldn't do and at the same time shorn of any real control. The rulers' dream of a society controlled almost entirely by the rich has been realised sooner than even the most optimistic of them can have imagined.

Many people who have detested this process are inclined to assume that all this has taken place because we have a Tory government. But the history outlined here has not corresponded to the governments in Whitehall. The years of greatest success for our side—1968 to 1973— straddled Labour and Tory governments. Our best year, 1972, fell right in the middle of a Tory government. However you measure it, in increased public investment, in trade union power and membership, in benefits paid out to the workers and the dispossessed, there has been no better year in all our history than 1972.

All these things happened against the promises and the intentions of the Tory government. They happened because our side used its strike power to roll back the Tory offensive and to go on the offensive ourselves. So determined was that effort that it eventually toppled the Tory government itself.

On the other hand some of the worst years from our point of view took place under a Labour government. Using the same measures as above, perhaps the worst year in all this period was 1976, under Labour.

The pattern of class struggle does not follow the pattern of elections or governments. The pillars of political and social history are not the general elections. They are the battles between the classes. On the one hand there is the smashing of the anti-trade union laws by trade union action in 1969 and 1972, the smashing of pay norms in 1972 and 1973, and the miners' strike of 1974. On the other hand we have seen the surrender to the employers in 1976 and 1977, the Ridley plan and the defeated strikes in steel, mining and printing of the 1980s.

The roots of change are not sunk in the change in control in Whitehall. They are sunk in offices, hospitals and factories where the real battle continues.

As long as they are in control of society, the rich and their Tory friends are engaged in a ceaseless, interminable effort to drive down our standard of living and to pulverise our organisations. They can only be stopped when we fight back.

The problem for the rich is that their victories on the class battlefield do not solve the contradictions and instabilities of their system. They have been winning pretty well continually since 1975. For much of that time, they have been trumpeting that their victories, and the defeat of the workers, will lead to universal prosperity. Soon after the miners' strike victory in 1985, someone in the Treasury invented a new phrase to describe the new economic miracle—the 'virtuous cycle', or 'virtuous circle'. The phrase became a favourite of chancellors of the exchequer. Nigel Lawson used it interminably, as did his successor, John Major.

33

The crushing of the unions and the privatising of public industry, it was alleged, had allowed private enterprise free rein. Gone was the suffocating influence of nationalisation and the 'halter' of trade union power. Now, employers were free to hire and fire at will and reduce wages to their 'true level'. There was nothing to prevent the economy ascending into a virtuous cycle in which low inflation would be followed by high investment and economic growth.

For a time, events seemed to prove these optimists right. The economy did grow almost uninterruptedly between 1985 and 1990. With the modesty of rich people throughout the ages, the Tories claimed that this was their work. Unleashed, the dynamism of the rich was enriching everyone. The huge increase in their own wealth would eventually 'trickle down' to the lower orders, who could then tug their forelocks in gratitude at the wonders of the rich men's world.

VIRGINIA BOTTOMLEY WARD CARE IN THE COMMUNITY UNIT

This is not satire, after the event. It was the profound and united conclusion of City of London forecasters all through 1987, 1988 and 1989. From the *Guardian*, to the *Independent* to the *Financial Times*, scholarly economics and financial correspondents predicted more and more of the virtuous cycle. Round and round we would go in a perpetual, ever expanding merry-go-round of growth and prosperity.

None of them predicted otherwise. Not one such expert, certainly no minister, not even a leading figure from Her Majesty's Opposition, predicted that in the summer of 1990, the British economy would grind to a halt, plunging the economy into an even longer recession than that of 1981. But that is what happened.

Before even the City economists could change their forecasts, before the words 'virtuous circle' died on

34

their lips, production and services suddenly stopped growing, discarding millions more on the dole and throwing the virtuously circling economy into reverse. The British economy shrank by 2 percent in 1991 and 3 percent in 1992.

This was not, as the Tory ministers constantly observe, just a British phenomenon. It was happening even more drastically in the United States, where the same policies of enriching the rich and impoverishing the workers had been carried out in the 'Reagan years' with tremendous enthusiasm. Average wages in the US in the 1980s were cut while the economy grew. The US rich feasted themselves on more and more tax cuts and perks. There too the whole process came to a juddering halt, stirring for the first time in 50 years a wave of resentment among American workers. The recession also took its toll in France, Germany and the other countries of Western Europe. In Russia and the east it engulfed millions of already impoverished people.

What did all this prove? It proved that even when the rich are winning in the tussle between the classes, they cannot overcome the intrinsic contradictions of their system. Indeed, in some ways the more successful they are in their class war, the more the contradictions in their system are exposed. The more they drive down wages, the less the people who receive wages can buy back the goods they produce. So even more people are thrown onto the dole rather than being allowed to produce things they need—and even fewer can afford to buy what they need at the prices demanded by the rich.

The more people on the dole, the more the government must borrow money to pay them to stay alive. The less the state spends on employing people in stable jobs in hospitals, schools and publicly-owned industry, the lower the revenue in taxes and therefore the more public spending has to be cut. Suddenly, the virtuous circle turns into a nightmare circle, leading to more and more poverty and destruction.

The capitalist system, the exploitative system for keeping the rich at the expense of the rest of the community, doesn't work. It cannot work. The flaws in it derive from its very essence: the exploitation of workers, the freedom of the market, and the division of the world's people into those who work for other peoples' benefit and those who benefit from other peoples' work. The contradictions which follow, the perennial slumps, cannot be overcome either without ending exploitation and the free market.

Those slumps are likely to get more and more severe. In post war Britain, each peak of unemployment has been higher or more sustained or both than the previous one. The breathing spaces in between (now known as 'recoveries') have been shallower and shallower. This is the reason why our children face an even worse world than ours.

The system, however, will not just disintegrate under the weight of its own contradictions and crises. The history of this century has shown that however desperate the capitalist crisis, however awful the measures needed to sustain it, the rich will hang on, literally like grim death.

They know that the end of their system is the end of their riches, their privileges, their high lifestyles and their right to rule. So they will resort to anything to stay in economic power. Above all, they will not surrender their power just because their system is in chaos.

Their world is rotten to the core, growing every day more rotten. The point, in Karl Marx's famous summary, is not just to analyse the world, expose its contradictions and wait for it to disintegrate. The point is to change it. But how?

36

The socialist answer

A S SOON as we see what's wrong with the capitalist system it's quite easy to see the alternative to it. Instead of capitalism, a system driven by the accumulation of wealth for the minority, we propose socialism, a system driven by the social needs of the majority of human beings. The basic elements of socialism arise quite naturally as the opposites of the absurdities of capitalism.

Planning

CAPITALISM depends on market forces which drive the owners of the means of production to compete with each other to produce according to where they can make a profit. Socialists insist on planning: that is, society deciding what to produce according to what people need and then according to what they want. The resources of society can't be planned unless the means of production which produce those resources are in public hands: that is, unless they are taken out of the hands of the rich.

This sounds obvious. But at once, thundering across the headlines for a century and more, come the objections.

'Public ownership is "grabbing" people's property'. *'These reds,'* shout the Tories and their allies, *'are after your possessions!'*

On the contrary, public ownership is not a threat to personal property at all. The socialist object is not, as is so often pretended, to take away people's personal property, to confiscate people's furniture, kitchen utensils,

37

washing machines and cars. Socialists want society to confiscate and control the means of producing all these things. One result, incidentally, will be that more personal property, the things people need and want, can and will be produced.

The only 'grabbing' which goes on in the socialist process is 'grabbing' from the greedy minority who have 'grabbed' from everyone else the means of producing the things they want and need (and which they do the work to produce).

'Planning is dictatorship. It is handing the economy to a bunch of bureaucrats who will decide what is produced by diktat.'

The first answer to this charge we've had already. It is that 'free enterprise' itself is dictatorship. The boards of multinational companies, for instance, who control most of the world's economy, decide what to produce, what prices to charge, who is to have jobs and who isn't—without consulting anyone, without a single vote being taken anywhere in their organisations. Indeed, all their organisations are designed so votes don't take place.

Secondly, is there really anything about planning which is essentially dictatorial? Suppose a group of people

WE'VE COME TO CUT DOWN YOUR BUREAUCRACY.

38

with a free afternoon at their disposal get together to plan how to spend their time. They would not like the matter to be decided by one of their number, and especially would not want that person to decide because he or she has the most money. They would all like to have their say, from which discussion would come a decision, a plan.

Similarly, an economic plan suggests not dictatorship but discussion and democracy. We all contribute, or have contributed, or will contribute to the economy. So we would all like to have a say, either directly or through representatives, in the priorities for that economy. It is the lack of a plan, rather than a plan, which ushers in dictatorship.

Equality

INSTEAD OF capitalist inequalities, socialism proposes equality. The essence of equality is that everyone gets from the society roughly the same.

Nothing causes the rich more indignation than this idea. Their indignation, so they tell us, has nothing to do with the possibility that they might lose their riches. What concerns them, they say, is that if people earn the same, they will all be the same. Equality, they argue, will lead to a grey sameness, to a stereotyped people all thinking and performing the same way, a drab, dull world such as that outlined in George Orwell's historic novel, *Nineteen Eighty Four*.

Our first answer is that most people nowadays earn the same or roughly the same anyway. In Britain, the vast majority of adults fall in a narrow band. 82 percent of taxpayers (21,709,000) got, before tax, between £100 and £400 a week in 1990-91. The rich, the only people who would lose a lot under a system of equality, are a tiny minority. 80,000 taxpayers—0.003% of the total—got £2,000 a week or more.

The second point is that sameness is a characteristic of capitalist society. A rigid education system which ends for most people at the age of 16 ensures that the majority has few cultural or intellectual aspirations. As a result, the masses read the same newspapers (the three most popular dailies in Britain are indistinguishable, and

39

sell between them 8 million copies every day), watch the same television, eat the same food and live in very much the same surroundings. A system of privilege and leisure only for a few leads to sameness among the many.

Equality is not sameness. In many ways it is its opposite. If people earn roughly speaking the same, they can then rise to the level of their own abilities and characteristics. Unhindered by the pressure 'to get on', to get more than their neighbour, they are far more likely to contribute to society in the way they most want to, and therefore in the way they know (and do) best.

Democracy

CAPITALISM is an essentially undemocratic system. It is based on a few people with money and power controlling the lives of the majority. Capitalist businesses are organised hierarchically, from the top down. Any attempt to seek out, let alone mobilise, the opinions of the mass of people is anathema to capitalists. Though they say they prefer a democratic system, they are quite happy when the government is a dictatorship.

Most of the countries of South America, for instance, are, or recently have been, run by the most dreadful dictatorships, but capitalism has got on there perfectly well. Indeed some of those dictatorships, like the one in Chile run for nearly 20 years by the dictator Pinochet, was ushered in and subsidised by capitalists.

The essence of socialism is that the product of human society should be controlled by society. It follows that socialism cannot survive without democracy. Its life blood is the involvement of the mass of the people.

How, for instance, can the socialist plan work unless those who are making the decisions day by day know what people want and what people can produce? Unless people can make their views felt, indeed unless the whole structure of society is essentially democratic, unless people are free constantly to challenge old ideas and provide new ones, a socialist plan cannot even be devised, let alone work in practice.

So if democracy means what it meant when the Greeks first introduced the word—the power of the

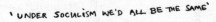
'UNDER SOCIALISM WE'D ALL BE THE SAME'

BOX D

people—it is an essential part of socialism. Any socialist government must be controlled from below, or it will not be a socialist government.

The problem with the word 'democracy' as it is used today is that it doesn't really mean 'the power of the people' at all. It means parliamentary democracy, a parliament elected by everyone voting at long intervals in geographical constituencies. That is one form of democracy, which, as we shall find out, is rather weak.

A socialist democracy would be based on democratically elected councils in workplaces, where most people spend most of their waking lives and where they have common interests and come together constantly in circumstances where they can share their opinions, argue or agree. Of course, there are a lot of people who do not work in workplaces, and they too need representation. Old people, people who work alone, child-carers, even children themselves can easily be grouped around each large work unit, and become part of the democratic process, arguing, voting, deciding with the people who work directly in it.

Nor is there any reason why a congress of workers' councils, the best form so far invented of socialist democracy, should not be reinforced or checked by a workers' council geographically elected.

We shall have a look at the record of parliamentary democracy in detail in a moment, but it couldn't be clearer from the very definition of socialism itself that democracy and democratic institutions are crucial to the

41

COMRADE
BOLOKOV
DEFENDER
OF THE
WORKERS'
REVOLUTIONARY
REPUBLIC CH.

survival of any socialist system.

What about Russia? Most people who have doubts about socialism ask this question. They say: 'Russia called itself socialist. So did Romania under the tyrant Ceaucescu and China under the brutes who ordered the 1989 massacre at Tiananmen Square.

'These countries had a "plan" didn't they? They said they believed in equality and workers' democracy. But they were plainly the most horrible tyrannies.' 'Frankly,' people conclude, 'if that's what socialism means, we might as well go on living under capitalism'.

Our argument is that these economies, led by Russia, were not planned at all. The 'plans' they boasted about, starting with the first Russian Five Year Plan in 1928, were not plans to make and distribute what people needed. Those plans did exactly the opposite. As in the West, they made people work harder and harder for less and less reward. As in the West, the priority was accumulation of wealth, at the expense of consumption. The pace and priorities of the plans were forced on Russia by her rulers' need to compete economically with the developed world. So they urged the workers, forced them, bullied, even tortured them to produce more.

Two things happened as a result. The people who did the bullying rapidly became a new ruling class, grabbing for themselves the surplus of what was produced.

TAKE THAT DOWN!

42

PRESIDENT
BOLOKOV
DEMOCRATICALLY
ELECTED
DEFENDER OF
FREE ENTERPRISE
& THE MARKET etc

The whole notion of equality was turned on its head.

Democracy was the other casualty. All semblance of dissent was ruthlessly squeezed out of Russia and the Eastern European countries. The decisions, political and economic, were taken by the same tightly-knit group of people who were syphoning off the surplus for their own use. A pattern of society emerged which was very similar to the society in the West. No planning to fit production to need, no equality and very definitely no democracy.

People and governments are always calling themselves something they aren't. Tory governments say they look after the common people, for instance. Tory ministers are always saying they care for people in need. No one is impressed by this, since they can see quite clearly that Tory governments couldn't care less about the common people. The point about Stalin's Russia and Ceaucescu's Romania is not what they said they were, but what they really were.

Since our foundation more than 30 years ago, the International Socialists and the Socialist Workers Party maintained that the economies of Russia, East Europe and China were not socialist—they were state capitalist. We argued that the essential characteristics of those societies—accumulation of wealth for the benefit of a minority, division of labour, hierarchical control of workplaces—

THAT'S BETTER!

43

were the same as in the West. The state played the role of the Western capitalist bosses.

Because we look at society from the point of view of the people who do the work, we found there was very little essential difference between the way things were produced and the way workers were dragooned in Russia and in private enterprise capitalist countries. It followed from this that the state capitalist countries were also plagued by internal contradictions. If you had a plan for production but didn't have the democracy to ensure that the production was organised for the mass of the people, then the same contradictions which drove private enterprise societies into crisis applied, even more strikingly, in Russia.

Though we argued this for 30 years and more, not one of us imagined that it would be vindicated quite so dramatically as it was in the late 1980s when the Russian and Eastern European state capitalisms literally disintegrated.

These arguments for socialism—planned economy, equality, workers' democracy—are not new. In one way or another, they have been put forward by prominent writers and politicians from all wings of the British Labour Party all through the century. How did the Labour Party put them into practice?

44

The Labour Party: passive socialism

WHEN IT STARTED, and for many decades afterwards, the Labour Party was proud to call itself socialist. The case for a planned economy was argued powerfully by men like GDH Cole, Harold Wilson, Sidney Webb, Evan Durban. RH Tawney wrote a marvellous book entitled *Equality*, and backed it up with an even more devastating argument against capitalism called *The Acquisitive Society*. In the 1930s Stafford Cripps and John Strachey argued for a complete break with the old capitalist order and the establishment by the next Labour government of a socialist society.

All these men were quite clear what was wrong with capitalist society. They despised the anarchy of the 'free market' and the inequalities and corruptions of capitalism. They were clear about the alternatives—planning and egalitarianism.

In 1918 Sidney Webb wrote the Labour Party constitution in which he defined the central purpose of the Labour Party as 'to secure for workers by hand or by brain the full fruits of their industry and the most equitable distribution thereof... upon the basis of the common ownership of the means of production.' There could not have been a plainer commitment to the policies of a planned economy to ensure a democratic and egalitarian socialist society.

45

Vagueness confused these people's ideas and writing only on the question of how capitalist society should be changed. Though they differed as to detail, they all agreed on the main instrument of change: parliament.

The formation of the Labour Party to represent working people in parliament and the winning of the vote for everyone—women over 30 first got the vote in 1918 and by 1930 all adults in Britain were able to vote—offered what they all believed was an 'obvious' route to change. The electorate must be persuaded to vote into parliament a Labour majority. Once that Labour majority was in, socialist legislation could be introduced. Since the workers by hand or brain were clearly the majority, there seemed no reason why that majority should not go on being re-elected until all the horrors of capitalism were eventually legislated out of existence.

The process, obviously, would be gradual. That was one of the attractions of it. There would be no violence, no shake-up of people's lives, just a gradual emancipation from exploitation and a steady improvement in workers' conditions.

How did this perspective work out? Before the Second World War there were two brief periods of Labour government, both utterly disastrous. The first, in 1924, lasted barely a year. The second, in 1929, was elected on a programme of ending unemployment (then about a million). By 1931, unemployment had tripled, and the government collapsed in disarray. Its leaders effectively joined the Tory Party, and helped to run a 'national government' committed to Tory policies. That last disaster plunged Labour into opposition all the way up to the war, when its leaders joined an all-party wartime coalition.

The collapse of the first two Labour governments did little to dampen the Labour Party socialists' faith in a future Labour government. Their undeniable argument was that both those governments had been in a minority in parliament, and had depended for their support on the Liberal Party, which, in classic Liberal tradition, had sided with the Tories when the going got rough.

46

After the war, it seemed that all the socialist hopes and propaganda of the previous 50 years had finally been realised. Angered by long years of war, and with their organisations strengthened by the full employment which the war effort demanded, workers were determined that there would be no return to poverty, unemployment and war. Though most Labour leaders wanted to continue with the coalition government, the rank and file of the party would have none of it. An election was called, which returned a Labour government with an enormous majority. In the next six years, the government did not lose a single by-election. Their support from the people was massive.

The new, huge parliamentary Labour Party sang the *Red Flag*. Hartley Shawcross, a young law officer in the new government, was reported to have declared: 'We are the masters now'. Many years later, when he became a Lord (and undoubtedly a master), he denied ever saying that. Certainly he and his colleagues, who included Stafford Cripps—later Chancellor of the Exchequer—and John Strachey, Minister of Food, did not seem in a special hurry to get the socialist society they had all argued for so passionately in the 1930s.

In a 1930s pamphlet, Cripps had argued that the next Labour government must break with that 'continuity of policy' which had destroyed it in 1924 and 1931. Yet 'continuity of policy' soon became the obsession of new Labour Ministers, including Cripps and Strachey.

For a time they maintained the old wartime controls, and even reconstructed them into permanent public ownership. The railways and the coal mines were nationalised. The National Health Service was created in the teeth of opposition from the doctors, though the Tory opposition was not fierce.

By 1947, when all the old arguments for a planned economy seemed to beckon the government to take over the main private industries, ministers seemed to back off. Harold Wilson, the young President of the Board of Trade, ordered a 'bonfire of controls' in which much of the old, egalitarian wartime controls were abandoned—in favour of private enterprise.

The rich, who had sunk to the depths of despair at the end of the war, got their breath and their confidence back. A barrage of 'free market' propaganda was un-

47

leashed against the Labour government. The voters still stayed loyal to Labour—more people voted for Labour or the Independent Labour Party (ILP) in the 1951 general election than ever before or since. But the Tories scraped in on the back of the collapsed Liberal Party.

Gone was the assumption that the reforms of Labour would sap the will of the ruling class, and that each Labour administration would spawn a new one, even more determined to change the system of society by getting hold of the economy and planning it. After six years of Labour government, British capitalism was revitalised, invigorated and confident enough to throw all its considerable efforts into prising out the Labour government.

The effect of all this on the socialist propagandists of the Labour Party was devastating. Cripps and Durbin had died. Tawney effectively stopped writing. Laski and Cole lost their socialist enthusiasm.

Strachey moved further and further to the right. In the 1930s and 1940s his pamphlet *Why You Should be a Socialist* had sold 1.5 million copies. Now, after his own practical experience of getting socialism through a Labour government, he started work on another book. It was published in 1956 and called *Contemporary Capitalism. Why You Should be a Capitalist* would have been as good a title.

His theme was that capitalism had been tamed by the strength of the Labour Party and by the trade unions. There was now no need for socialist politicians to talk

48

about changing the nature of society. There was full employment, economic growth, a welfare state. What was left except to make society better, gradually?

The same theme was endorsed much more stridently in a fashionable book published the same year by Anthony Crosland, a young devotee of the new leader of the Labour Party, Hugh Gaitskell. Crosland too called for 'practical politics', an end to the ideology of the left, and a concentration of control of the economy by Labour governments not through owning the means of production but by using financial measures to guide it in the right direction.

When Labour lost the 1959 election, Crosland's book was quoted all over the place as the intellectual case for chucking Clause Four, committing Labour to the common ownership of the means of production, distribution and exchange. This was the strong view of Gaitskell, his deputy George Brown, and many of the Labour leaders.

The rank and file of the party saved Clause Four, and Gaitskell died in 1963. The new leader of the party, Harold Wilson, a consummate master of the politician's art of saying one thing and doing another, kept the words of Clause Four but spent the next 13 years, during most of which time he was prime minister, leading his party away from it.

In 1964, against a background of full employment, growth in the economy and a corrupt Tory government, the Labour Party overturned a Tory majority of nearly 100 and came back to office. Seventeen months later, in March 1966, Labour was returned with a majority of nearly 100. It was the high peak of electoral achievement of the British Labour Party. There seemed to be few limits to the reforming potential represented by this vast new majority.

Yet within months the whole of that reforming policy was thrown into reverse. In the election campaign, Wilson had spoken derisively of the Tories' 'one-sided pay pause'. He introduced, in the summer of 1966, a wage freeze—enforceable by law and utterly 'one-sided'. With the wage freeze went a whole host of proposals for public

49

spending cuts which reversed Labour's slogans of both election campaigns. All this was done ostensibly to avoid the devaluation of the pound. Yet in 1967, the pound was devalued to be followed by still more freezing and cuts.

The socialist jewel in the crown of the Labour government—the issue which had forced Wilson himself to resign from the Labour government in 1951—the free health service, re-established in the first flush of electoral victory in 1964, was now breached.

Negotiations were opened with the International Monetary Fund, the guardians of international capitalism, for a loan. The IMF insisted as part of the loan's conditions that charges should be re-imposed on health service prescriptions. The amount of money raised by this charge was minimal, a tiny fraction of the huge sums negotiated. Wilson and his negotiators held out for the free health service, knowing that their supporters treasured this prize of modern labour above all others. The IMF were adamant, and the charges were levied. The effect on the morale of Labour Party activists who had hailed their party's electoral success with such joy and hope only three months earlier, was catastrophic.

Labour lost the election of 1970, leaving the Tories in for another four years. When Wilson returned to Downing Street at the head of another minority government in March 1974, the old process started again. Labour's programme for the election had been even more radical than in 1964 and 1966. Its principal promise was 'Back to Work with Labour', a pledge to end the menace of mass dole queues which under the Tories, for the first time since the war, had reached a million. Despite a second election in 1974, which gave Labour a parliamentary majority, unemployment rose inexorably to one and a half million.

When Labour, under a new leader and Prime Minister, James Callaghan, finally left office in 1979, unemployment was twice as high as it was when Labour was first returned. There had been more talks with the IMF, resulting in another big loan—and more cuts in public services, including the National Health Service.

50

The consistent theme of British Labour in the century since it was formed has been the slippage in its socialist aspirations. The slippage continued in the long years of opposition after the crushing defeat of 1979. The more Labour lost at the polls, the more its leaders shied away from the socialist commitments which had brought many of them into politics in the first place.

The central achievement of Neil Kinnock, who became Labour Party leader in 1983, and left the post in 1992, during which time Labour lost two general elections, was the removal from Labour Party policy of any commitment to rid Britain of nuclear weapons.

Though Kinnock had been a passionate supporter of the Campaign for Nuclear Disarmament, he strove might and main, with great success, to shift his party away from the policy in which he personally believed.

Since 1992, when Kinnock was replaced by a leader from the conventional right of the party, John Smith, the process has continued apace. As this is written, the new leadership is engaged in a desperate fight to cut the ties with the trade unions which brought Labour into existence in the first place. They want their party cleared of the remotest connection with anything which smells of class.

At the same time the remnant of an economic policy which challenged the hegemony of the rich is also being jettisoned. The milk and water 'interventionism' of the 1950s, 1960s and even 1970s is now regarded as too left wing, too frightening for the electorate. The language of egalitarianism and a planned economy is being expunged from speeches by the leadership. Smith and his two main lieutenants, Gordon Brown and Tony Blair, talk about individualism, ambition and being a party in which people who succeed in society can feel at home.

As the crisis of capitalism becomes more and more acute, so the Labour leaders seem more and more anxious not to talk about it. At the Labour Party conference of 1990, Smith (then the party's spokesperson on the economy) held out two remedies for the unpredicted recession which had suddenly overcome British industry: join the European Exchange Rate Mechanism and lower interest rates by 1 percent. The following week, at their conference, the Tory leaders announced that they were

51

joining the ERM and lowering interests rates by 1 percent. When the whole ERM policy collapsed in ruins in September 1992, there was nothing the Labour leader Smith could say about it since it was his policy which had collapsed as well.

What was happening to Labour's socialism? It was disappearing.

Socialism, both the word and the idea, had been the proud boasts of the early Labour pioneers, including the most reactionary of them. In 1923, the parliamentary Labour Party under its right wing leader Ramsay Macdonald, put down a motion calling for the establishment in Britain of a socialist society. The motion was lost but the leaders continued to describe socialism as their objective.

Macdonald's successors as leader, not just the left winger Lansbury, but the right wingers Attlee, Gaitskell, Wilson and Callaghan, all spoke enthusiastically about socialism. When Neil Kinnock was elected leader in 1983 he told the Labour Party conference in his acceptance speech: 'We have to commend the common sense of socialism, the realism of socialism, for that is how we get the maxim for socialism—the most rational, reasonable, emancipating creed ever put on the agenda of humankind for the advancement of humankind.'

Gradually the word sunk from his vocabulary. What the Labour leaders had achieved in practice was eventually reflected in their language. Socialism, like public ownership and equality and unilateral disarmament, joined the long list of words which are expected to frighten the electorate. They cannot be used, even late in the evening.

So now, at a time when the capitalist system itself is proving the case for the socialist alternative more powerfully than at any other time this century, the leaders of the Labour Party fall over themselves to disassociate their party from anything which has about it the slightest whiff of socialism.

Why and how has this happened? Why haven't Labour been able to use their power as elected governments to roll back the awful march of the rich?

There are two answers, both dependent on one another and both of which go back to the division of our society into classes.

The weakness of parliament

AS WE'VE seen, the rich gang together as a class. They create a machinery of the state to protect their property. Of course, they don't call this machinery the 'protection of the rich brigade'. One of the great strengths of this machinery is that it pretends to be neutral. Thus we are told that the police are neutral, the judges are neutral, the civil servants are neutral, the army and intelligence services are neutral, the press is free. But in fact, as can be shown by countless examples, these institutions are all run by rich and privileged people for rich and privileged people. They like to appear to be fair and rational and even handed, but where their interests and their prestige conflict with even handedness they become ruthlessly irrational and unfair.

For the last 100 years their narrow, secret and unaccountable hierarchy has had to cope with a system of political democracy through which parliaments and local councils are elected by everyone. The capitalist hierarchy bitterly resisted political democracy when it was first mooted. In the late 1830s, for instance, millions of people signed a petition called the Charter calling for votes for all men and regular parliaments. The Chartists' movement was supported by working class people who openly expressed their hatred and contempt for the rich. The rich were terrified by it. They threw the whole resources of their state against the Charter, and the Chartists were defeated. 20 years later, bit by bit, and always remaining in control, the rich started to

DESIGNER SOCIALISM OR NOT IN POWER DRESSING.

53

grant the vote to the workers. First in 1867, then in 1884, skilled male workers with a bit of property got the vote. Then, in 1918, women over 30 and unskilled workers got the vote too. For the last 70 years or so, almost all adults in this country have had the right to vote.

The argument among the rulers went like this. There is a huge demand for the vote, which we cannot resist forever. If we do resist it, the workers will eventually rise in revolution. Perhaps, if we give it bit by bit and are seen to be giving it rather than having it taken from us, we can contain the democracy which the vote represents. Thus at the peak of confidence and expansionism in nineteenth century capitalism, the workers were granted the vote piecemeal.

How did the rich ever believe they could survive once the vote was granted? Many believed they couldn't. Others, more progressive, felt that electoral democracy could be contained within the system: that capitalist hierarchies could survive side by side with elected governments, because the democracy which elected the governments could easily be humbled, bribed, bullied and contained by the hierarchies.

How could they be so impudently confident? How could they imagine they could continue in charge even when the prime minister and government of the country owed their office to the electorate? The chief reason was that they could detect that the democracy of an elected parliament was pathetically weak.

Parliamentary democracy is based on voting by geography: you vote according to where you live. Where people live does have some relevance to where they are in the class divide. Sections of cities are rich areas, others are working class areas.

The electoral map often follows these class divisions. But electoral constituencies often include people of completely different class interests, whose economic interests are incompatible. Most MPs find they have to represent the interests of rich and poor, employer and employed, landlord and tenant. The conflicting interests often make effective representation impossible. Most MPs respond by concentrating on those of their constituents

54

with the greatest clout—almost invariably the rich and their acolytes.

Then there is the inequality of the voting system itself. 'One person, one vote' sounds very fair and reasonable and so it would be in a society where people were getting roughly the same. But when a salaried printworker has one vote and another man, his proprietor, a media boss with five newspapers and millions of pounds in the bank also has one vote, are these men equally represented in society?

Of course not. The mogul with one vote wields far greater power in the society, including the power to hire and fire the printworker, whose vote cannot save him from the sack. The fact that two people of different wealth and power are represented by one vote makes a mockery of the notion of equal representation, yet there are thousands of such examples in every constituency.

The power from below is further weakened by the infrequency of voting. Most people will vote for a parliament perhaps eight times in their lives. The long periods in between votes weakens the connection between the representative and the represented. The only demand of the Chartists which hasn't been fulfilled is the demand for annual parliaments. This demand was included quite deliberately in the Chartists' programme in order to avoid the possibility that MPs might become remote from their electorate, arrogant in office and insensitive to what the people who so irregularly elect them are thinking about their performance.

To this is added the remoteness and majesty of parliament. Aneurin Bevan, when he first went to parliament in 1929, said the place was dedicated to 'ancestor worship'. MPs are made to feel important by the rulers, so long as they do not try to appear important to their electors. The constant pull of the ruling class—the fully-paid lobbyists, the glamorous surroundings, the quaint procedures, the importance of tradition, the availability of 'consultancies' in which, increasingly, capitalist enterprises buy their MP—weakens the link between the elector and the elected and correspondingly weakens the power of labour to be represented in capitalist society.

The vote was conceded, then, not without some anguish, in the hope that capitalists could hang on to their power side by side with a parliamentary democracy: that the parliaments would be so weak that they would never seriously challenge the undemocratic power and wealth of the rich. This uneasy co-existence has gone on through most of the twentieth century without too much trouble for the rich. Of course, they still detest democracy, especially where it threatens to take what they regard as theirs and hand it over to the poor.

When the Greater London Council appeared it might provide services for the poor and the dispossessed, the Tory government abolished it. Similarly, the powers of local councils have been consistently abused and subverted by the Tories.

Nationalised industries, the creatures of parliament and accountable to parliament, have been privatised and thus removed from public accountability. But even where they existed they were deprived of the same sort of rights to take part in the market as private enterprises enjoyed.

Precisely because it hasn't presented any real threat to the rich, parliament has been tolerated throughout the century. Every time Labour governments have moved even momentarily in the direction of weakening capitalist power or towards egalitarianism, they have been obstructed, abused and halted in their tracks by the combined power of the undemocratic state.

The examples after a century of intermittent Labour governments are legion. When the most recent Labour government tried to impose a petroleum revenue tax of 90 percent, the oil industry in the North Sea went on an investment strike and brought the tax rate down below 50 percent. Thus, at a swoop, it ensured that billions of pounds otherwise available for hospitals and schools remained in the greedy and tightly controlled hands of the oil industry directors.

When post office workers (affiliated to the Labour Party) tried to carry out their own union policy and ban post to racist South Africa, the High Court intervened and told them they couldn't. The same thing happened when

Labour Party education policy was imposed on a selective school in Tameside.

In 1987 three Labour Ministers (right wingers all) stood on a picket line at Grunwicks in North London where Asian women workers were being refused their right to join a trade union. But when the anti-union management held its ground and took pickets to court, the Labour government's own new union laws were powerless to help the Grunwicks workers.

All through all the Labour governments the tussle between the democratically elected government and the ruling class was consistently won by the rulers. No wonder the rulers feel so confident of co-existence with parlia-

THE EMPEROR'S NEW CLOTHES

mentary democracy that they now praise it as though they had invented it. Their system remains as undemocratic as ever but the history of 100 years of parliamentary democracy has threatened them so little that they are prepared to identify their undemocratic system with parliamentary democracy.

Does this mean that we should be against parliamentary democracy? Sometimes new socialists, as they suddenly appreciate the weakness and sham of parliamentary democracy, denounce it root and branch. They say that 'it doesn't matter' whether we have a parliamentary democracy or not. This is plain foolishness. Parliamentary

57

democracy is an incalculable improvement on a system where there is no democracy at all. The right to hold socialist meetings and publish socialist papers, for instance, derives from parliamentary democracy. A parliament with a right to question and control the executive creates a certain space for socialist argument and socialist organisation. Any successful effort to cut down democracy—like the abolition of the GLC or the Inner London Education Authority, or the constant 'capping' and controlling of Labour councils—brings with it more reactionary and more extensive attacks on the workers.

Thus socialists defend parliamentary democracy and all its forms against fascists and bureaucrats who seek to curtail it. But that does not deflect us at all from continuing to attack parliamentary democracy because it leaves the power of the rulers intact. It gives the appearance of a democracy without being able to confront or change the undemocratic capitalist powers which control society. Lenin summed up his indignation in typically forthright style, when he wrote that parliamentary democracy 'always remains, and under capitalism is bound to remain, restricted, truncated, false and hypocritical, a paradise for the rich and a snare and deception for the exploited, for the poor... deceipt, violence, corruption, mendacity, hypocrisy and oppression of the poor is hidden beneath the civilised, polished and perfumed exterior of modern bourgeois democracy.'

Passivism

THE REAL argument against Labour and its faith in parliamentary democracy is that it tends to weaken our side in the perpetual struggle with the rich.

If you believe that society must and will be changed through parliament, it follows that in general it is better to leave politics to the parliamentary politicians. If the central political aim is to return a Labour MP to parliament, the logic of the parliamentary system means that you should leave political decisions to the MP.

Being an MP becomes a profession. People talk about 'going into politics' as if it were chartered surveying or medicine.

The professionals, the players, are the people actually doing the job in parliament. The spectators are the supporters in the constituencies. The professionals like the cheering of the spectators, but they are irritated if the crowd tries to get on the pitch. Their message is that people should 'leave us alone to make up our own minds and do what we think is best'. All forms of political activity outside parliament are discouraged by this process.

One result has been a startling decline in Labour Party membership, which reached over a million in 1952, and has declined progressively ever since. Today there are probably no more than 250,000 Labour Party members. What do they do? A recent survey found that 50 percent of Labour members now do nothing at all about their membership. The enormous majority of the rest spend less than an hour a week on political activity.

The way the Labour Party is organised encourages this passivity. It is based on constituencies, linked only to the electoral process. The timing of Labour Party life is dominated not by real political developments but by conferences which discuss resolutions submitted many months before the debates. The tempo of political organisation and discussion is entirely removed from the tempo of everyday life, especially the tussle between the classes.

Strikes, for instance, have always embarrassed the Labour Party. Though the trade unions came together to form the Labour Party in 1900, they went along with the prevailing view of the Labour leaders that strikes were embarrassing and should be kept to a minimum. This theory prevailed on the right and left of the early Labour Party.

Ramsay Macdonald, when leader of the party, wrote a book *Socialism and Syndicalism*, which argued that strikes were a menace to the forward march of Labour. On the left wing, Bruce Glasier of the Independent Labour Party, argued again and again—he wrote whole pamphlets on this single theme—that the 'political' (that is, the parliamentary) work of the new Labour Party was disrupted by strikes. The best thing strikers could do for the good of the Labour Party, urged Glasier, was to go back to work.

People like Glasier took the argument even further

59

to suggest that strikes were the last resort of the lumpen proletariat while civilised workers looked for change through parliament. These theories have grown in strength and effectiveness as the century has proceeded.

The Labour leaders pretended not to notice the General Strike of 1926. When they did notice, they strove mightily, and successfully, to sell the strike out at any price. The Labour government of 1945-1951 ruthlessly broke strikes, especially in the docks.

The great miners' strikes of 1972 and 1974 were intensely embarrassing to the Labour leaders, who constantly begged their supporters to 'remain constitutional'.

Now, at the end of the century, the whole process reaches its logical conclusion. Labour asks the trade unions to disaffiliate from the party they formed, and urges party members to settle arguments of their representatives not, as in the past, by meeting together, arguing and discussing things as comrades, but by voting in isolation by postal ballot, where the only real advice and argument comes from the television set.

Passivity in politics is utterly destructive of the health and strength of the working class movement.

In the early days, when the vote had to be won from the Liberals, Labour sponsored education classes where workers could learn about things which formal education had never taught them and never would. Working class libraries and institutes were set up. A rich variety of books, newspapers, magazines and pamphlets were circulated regularly by Labour and the ILP. After a century of passive politics, all this is now ancient history. The libraries have been sold off to book dealers, the institutes wound up, the papers folded. The Labour Party now has no newspaper. The Trades Union Congress, which once ran the biggest-circulation daily paper in the country, the *Daily Herald*, sold the paper off in 1958. It is now Rupert Murdoch's *Sun*.

What kind of new society do our modern parliamentary reformers hope to build out of all this passivity? How do they imagine any kind of socialist order being created from above, when the people who are expected to benefit from it are sullen, passive, reading the *Sun* and the *Mirror* and watching interminable trash on the television? Passivity leads not to any form of new social order, but backwards towards reaction, racism and despair. The power our side has to change society—the power to organise to challenge society with our own power, especially our industrial power, is consistently weakened by the parliamentary process, and the belief that politics begins and ends in Labour Party conferences and general elections.

The awful consequences of passivity loom like a cloud over the period in which this pamphlet is written. In October 1992, the Tory government announced the closure of half the coal mining industry. They were quite unprepared for the tidal wave of rage and indignation that swept the country. Huge, furious demonstrations forced them to postpone their plans. The demand suddenly arose, spontaneously and quite genuinely, for a general strike to save the mining industry. There was nothing unrealistic about this demand. In 1972, a general strike call from the TUC had in effect broken the entire industrial strategy of the Conservative government.

The reaction in 1992 from official Labour was immediate. Norman Willis, general secretary of the TUC, who has been cooling off like a giant fish on a slab ever since he became a full time union official after leaving college 30 years ago, said: 'we need a cooling off period'.

Parliamentary Labour took his advice. They diverted the national fury into the Select Committee rooms at Westminster (where they were anyway in a minority). Unhappily, the movement followed them. There was no call from the union leaders for industrial action. The demonstrations petered out. The Parliamentary Committees reported—and were ignored.

When everybody had cooled off, the government closed down the mining industry. The parliamentary road led to disaster. Yet the alternative—a general strike in October—would have rescued and re-invigorated the mining industry as certainly as it was rescued and re-invigorated by the great miners' strikes of 1972 and 1974.

Many people see and understand what happened that October, have nothing but contempt for the abject

61

surrender of the trade union and Labour leaders. They are sick to death of weak leadership which tells us to concentrate on our weaknesses, not our strengths.

They want to stop the long retreat of Labour and the union leaders and to place again on the agenda the overwhelming case for socialism. But how?

The socialist party: active socialism

ARE WE doomed forever to pay homage to people like John Monks and Gordon Brown? Is there an alternative?

Yes, there is. The alternative can be found every day, in almost every city and town, however terrible the times we live in. The alternative is the people who are prepared to resist, to fight back.

What sort of people? Well, people like the anti-poll tax protesters who said 'enough is enough'—and went on to build a movement which sank the Tories' flag ship and destroyed Margaret Thatcher's premiership. Or the teachers and parents whose combined opposition sank the Tories' next flag ship policy—a huge burden of new education testing.

In less publicised circumstances handfuls of people in every factory and workplace have called on their colleagues to stand up to union-busting, sackings and speed-up. Sometimes they have won, often they have lost, but their spirit of defiance and their will to fight back stood between the workforce and surrender.

As I write this, a fascist has been elected as councillor in East London. This shocking fact has inspired

63

thousands of people all over the country to organise resistance to the fascists. Some have started arranging coaches for a demonstration to close down the British National Party headquarters. Some have swarmed down to Brick Lane in London on Sunday mornings to knock the fascists off their perch. Others have resolved to argue all the more fiercely whenever a single sign of racism appears in arguments at work.

Near where I live they propose to cut through a dense working class housing area with a motorway which few local people will want to use. At the same time the cross-London rail service which takes so many to work a few miles from their home are threatened with closure. A giant campaign has started to save the railways and ditch the road.

In almost every area of the country campaigns have been started to save the environment, to keep hospitals open, to stop another hyper-market gobbling up more of the countryside, to clear the seas and rivers of chemical pollution and sewage, to put an end to the perpetual silent menace of nuclear power.

Like the strikers, the militant workers and the anti-Nazi campaigners, all these people are leaders of revolt. Their anger and their conviction pushes them into giving a lead to others to do something to resist.

Every one of them has noticed that resistance of the kind they have tried to inspire succeeds in changing the people who take part. So often you hear the potential reformer moaning: 'how can we change the world when there is so much racism and sexism?' Such moaners are, quite rightly, not very impressed by the suggestion that change will come from the next Labour government which will pass another law against racism and sexism. These laws don't change how people think and feel. But resistance in the struggle, especially in strikes, does change the way people think.

Everyone who has been involved in any kind of strike has been amazed at the change which comes over the people who take part. In the great miners' strike of 1984-85, everyone noticed the astonishing social transformation of the mining villages. Two centuries of su-

64

perstition about masculine superiority were swept aside in a few weeks.

When people take action themselves in defiance of their boss or their state, they get a whiff of their own capacity, their own intelligence, their own independent character. They feel confident. Confidence brings contempt for all the rotten prejudices which distracted their attention while they grovelled to the bosses and obeyed their rules.

Always there are people determined to resist. Always their resistance brings them into confrontation with the rich and, in the process, makes them into socialists of one kind or another.

Their resistance, moreover, relates to something which is happening, the solution to which demands some kind of action now. It cannot wait until the next election. All these people who fight back feel the need for solidarity. Lack of solidarity is usually the main reason why they don't get as far as they hoped.

The overwhelming need is to unite all these resisters into a single organisation.

The rich are always seeking to divide the resisters, to pack them off into separate containers—'green campaigner', 'gay rights activist', 'industrial militant', 'nuclear disarmer'. Yet each campaign, each resistance, depends for its success and its credibility on the links it can forge with others who are also being pushed about and exploited.

The rich are seeking always to strengthen their class ties with their supporters in the law, the police, the media. We need to unite all our supporters too. To be strong enough to take them on we cannot rely on five independent fingers, all of them weak. We need the strength of the fist.

What sort of organisation can link all these re-

65

sisters? Can it be just a loose federation of militants who pool their enthusiasm and their strength?

No, it must be more than that. Our opponents—the union bashers, the racists, the welfare cutters—are much better organised than that. They plan and think and recall past battles. So must we.

We need our own history—the exact opposite of the ridiculous history we are taught in schools.

We need to know not the names and dates of monarchs but the stories of the struggles against those monarchs. We need to know about the Levellers, the Chartists, the Irish Land League, the New Trade Unionism, the dock strike of 1889, the 1926 General Strike, the Unemployed Workers Movement of the 1930s.

We need to know about the great revolutions, not from the familiar point of view of executed or abdicated tyrants but from the point of view of the poor, the illiterate and the hungry.

We need to know about the few times in history when workers did run society, about the Paris Commune of 1871, the early years of the Russian Revolution, about the workers' committees in Kiel and Munich in 1918 and 1919, Turin in 1920, Budapest in 1956, Paris in 1968, Lisbon in 1975, Teheran in 1979.

We need to know what revolutions can do, and why they have so often been defeated. We cannot learn these lessons individually, just by reading books at home. We need to keep our history and our memory alive by constant discussion among ourselves, freed by our solidarity from reactionary text-books foisted upon us at school and college.

We need our own newspapers. We cannot expect to mount an effective assault on the society of the rich while we are reading, exclusively, their newspapers and watching their television.

It is no good hoping to launch our own newspapers on the 'free market'. The vast media monopolies, up to half of their revenue financed by advertising and utterly in control of the distribution network, do not take kindly to socialist newspapers. We need our own, but we will not get them if people who hate the world we live in stay at home and keep their own company. If socialist newspapers are to circulate they have to be sold, hand to hand. They need not only the journalists and print workers who produce them but a whole army of people who will then go out and sell them.

We need politics: political organisation, socialist organisation.

You can't be a socialist on your own. That sounds so obvious it is almost embarrassing to write it down. Yet still the world is full of people who declare they are socialists and then confess they are on their own.

Socialism is a system of society founded on co-operation, on pooling and sharing our resources. Getting socialism requires even more sharing and pooling. We cannot even start to change the world unless all those who want to do so help to build a socialist organisation.

The Socialist Workers Party is such an organisation. It is effectively the only British socialist organisation of any size which seeks to organise people on the basis of active resistance to capitalism.

The pace and tempo of the SWP is entirely different to that of the Labour Party. Labour wants to change society through parliament, so they concentrate their efforts on elections. As a result, participation in politics except at election times is positively discouraged.

We concentrate our efforts on the people who are fighting and are prepared to fight. This struggle sets the timetable of our activity. We seek constantly to expand

67

The socialist party

our political understanding, our knowledge of history, our newspapers so that we can encourage the resistance to capitalism.

Our central slogan is the first sentence which Karl Marx wrote when he set out the aims of the International Working Men's Association, that the emancipation of the working class must be the act of the working class itself. Slavery was not abolished by the slave-owners, nor (despite our historians) by comfortable reformers such as Wilberforce. The slaves emancipated themselves. Similarly, workers will not be emancipated by their bosses, nor by reformers who co-operate with those bosses. Workers can and will only emancipate themselves, but it will not do so unless we build inside the labour movement a socialist leadership which can point the way.

Many socialists who agree with us about so much are reluctant to join. Some still stay loyal to a Labour Party which is increasingly impatient of any socialist membership. For most, the real stumbling block is the image of SWP members as they are portrayed in the media: unthinking fanatics. But SWP members are not born socialists. We all became socialists because we were persuaded by an argument, an act of defiance, an example. We have survived through the years when so many other socialist organisations have disappeared precisely because we never believed we were separate from or more important than the mass of the working class.

If we appear more confident and articulate, this is not because we are more able, more fanatical or even more committed. Nor is it because we all devote our entire lives to party membership. Our members are not sent from some other planet to devote every moment to subverting the system. We are workers, sons and daughters, mothers and fathers, music-lovers and music-haters, sports-lovers and sports-haters, with too much (or too little) work to do, and too many bills to pay—just like everyone else.

Some of us contribute a lot to the party, some of us a little. All of us have friends outside the party and we wouldn't be any good as socialists if we didn't. If we seem confident, it is not because of single-mindedness or fanaticism. It is because, by pooling our resources, we have

the tools to do the job. We can call demonstrations and know that at least some people will go on them. We can produce leaflets and newspapers, knowing that lots of people will sell them and distribute them. We can promise help to strikers knowing that we have a network of workers who will hear their case and stump up what they can. And in the midst of the struggle we look at the history and ideas of the socialist movement so that we can emulate the successes and avoid repeating the defeats. The knowledge, the struggle and the solidarity give us the kind of confidence that a lone socialist lacks.

Not enough though. Nothing like enough. Every week, the gap between what we should be doing and what we can do grows wider.

The whole world is, in the poet Shelley's words, 'pining in pain'. Riven by their own chaos and corruption, the rulers are poised for another mighty lurch to the right. The memory of fascism returns to Europe in a series of awful flashbacks: millions of fascist votes in France, a barbaric civil war in Bosnia, the charred bodies of the victims of racist attacks in Germany.

On our side there are plenty of signs of rage and horror. Both explode all the time like fireworks, lighting up the sky for a few moments and then fizzling out. While Labour slinks off to the right and the union leaders prevaricate, a huge empty space opens out on the left.

We could fill that space, if we were stronger. We

69

The socialist party

could stop the reaction in its tracks and turn it round—if only the people who say they are socialists decide that now is the time to do something about it.

We need thousands more active socialists. Hundreds of thousands.

On our own, we can sit at home and moan about the world.

Together, we can change it.

Other publications
from Bookmarks

Guides to socialism

How Marxism Works
Chris Harman
An outstanding explanation of the main themes of Marxist thought.
£2.50, 96pp

The Revolutionary Ideas of Karl Marx
Alex Callinicos
Over a century since Marx analysed capitalism as a system prone to recession and wars, this book shows his ideas to be as relevant today.
£3.95, 208pp

Arguments for revolutionary socialism
John Molyneux
Any socialist faces a barrage of questions, from human nature to overpopulation. This is an invaluable guide to the answers.
£3.50, 128pp

The Changing Working Class
Alex Callinicos and Chris Harman
Are today's white collar workers really middle class? Has the traditional manual working class disappeared? What about the 'underclass'?
£3.95, 106pp

What is the real Marxist Tradition?
John Molyneux
Explodes the myth that social democracy and Stalinism have anything to do with socialism and searches for the genuine tradition.
£2.50, 80pp

Socialism: Utopian and Scientific
Frederick Engels
Still one of the best short guides to what the struggle for socialism is really all about.
Engels links the fight for the future to the shape of the present society. In doing so he builds a stable bridge that links our hopes and endeavours of today with the struggle for a better world.
£2.95, 128pp

Other titles

Crime, Class and Corruption: the Politics of the Police
Audrey Farrell
This examination of the real roots of crime finds the police
have no role in stopping it, and instead hold up a system
that gives rise to crime in the first place.
£5.95, 208pp

The Labour Party: a Marxist History
Tony Cliff and Donny Gluckstein
Where the Labour Party comes from, how it is thwarted in
government and what lies behind the current race for
respectability.
£7.95, 432pp

Trotsky's Marxism
Duncan Hallas
The best short introduction to the ideas of this great socialist.
£3.50, 122pp

Malcolm X: Socialism and Black Nationalism
Kevin Ovenden
A best seller, unravelling the life of Malcolm X against the
turbulent background of the US in the 1950s and 1960s. A
critical examination of what Malcolm X offers the struggle
today.
£2.95, 96pp

Killing the Nazi Menace
Chris Bambery
How to fight the fascists—drawn from the experience of the
1930s and the 1970s.
£1.50, 48pp

Sex, Class and Socialism
Lindsey German
Women now have far greater control over their lives than
ever before, yet their oppression persists. Lindsey German
analyses how the family shapes women's lives under
capitalism.
£5.95, 256pp

Abortion: A woman's right to choose
Ruth Brown
The whys and hows of fighting for abortion rights.
£2.00, 40pp

Ireland's Permanent Revolution
Chris Bambery
The starting point of this book, now in its third edition, is that Britain created the mess in Ireland and should therefore get out now. But it goes further than this and argues for a strategy to unite workers North and South in a struggle to get rid of the border and fight for socialism.
£3.50, 128pp

The Fire Last Time: 1968 and After
Chris Harman
The year which rocked rulers from Paris to Prague, Berkeley to Berlin. Why the explosion occurred and how it eventually fizzled out.
£6.95, 416pp

Nicaragua: What went wrong
Mike Gonzalez
Traces the road from the Sandinistas' 1979 insurrection to electoral defeat in 1990.
£4.50, 144pp

Israel: the Hijack State
John Rose
The origins of Zionism, its significance to imperialism and the resistance it has sparked.
£2.50, 80pp

South Africa between Apartheid and Capitalism
Alex Callinicos
Interviews with leading figures on the South African left, compiled as the country stands at the crossroads.
£5.95, 192pp

BOOKMARKS

265 Seven Sisters Road, London N4 2DE
PO Box 16085, Chicago, Il. 60616
GPO Box 1473N, Melbourne 3001

Why you should join the socialists